FLEET

Judith Willson has worked as a teacher
and in publishing. Her work was featured
in Carcanet's *New Poetries VI* and her
first collection, *Crossing the Mirror Line*,
was published by Carcanet in 2017. She
grew up in London and Manchester
and now lives in the Yorkshire Pennines.

Fleet

JUDITH WILLSON

CARCANET

First published in Great Britain in 2021 by
Carcanet
Alliance House, 30 Cross Street
Manchester M2 7AQ
www.carcanet.co.uk

A CIP catalogue record for this book is
available from the British Library.

ISBN 978 1 80017 024 7

Book design by Andrew Latimer
Printed in Great Britain by SRP Ltd, Exeter, Devon

The publisher acknowledges financial
assistance from Arts Council England.

CONTENTS

The Parrot-Keeper's Guide, by an Experienced Dealer 7
The ornithology gallery 8
West India Dock 10
Bird dealer's wife 11
The London Cage 12
A map of roads and navigable waters 13
Required to appear 14
Children's song (*my father whistled to the river*) 16
The tune he heard on Vinegar Street 17
Children's song (*when my father spoke*) 18
The prisoner said 19
A demonstration 21
Eliza in the laundry 22
Children's song (*my father wore translated shoes*) 23
Women dancing in a circle 24
I press my eye to a paper peepshow 26
Eliza, old 27
Children's song (*two birds sat on a white stone*) 28
Disappearances 29
Signature 30
Writing backwards to the birdcage maker 32

Haunting Eliza 33

In the marsh country
Map 41
Fleet, high tide, 10 pm 42
Old Hall Marshes 43
Fingringhoe, St Margaret of Antioch 44
Bradwell Power Station (decommissioned) 45
Pillbox 46
Dengie 47

Southend   48
Rotherhithe   49
Either an eyepiece or a correcting lens   52
The human voice from a distance   53
In early photographs, busy streets appear deserted 54
Transit circle   55
Zugunruhe   57
A map of the world   58
A story   59
Goldfinches   60
Silver plating, gilding, restoration to new life 61
Fincantieri   63
About time   64
Corset shop window in the East End   66

Notes   69
Acknowledgements   71

FLEET

DESERTING CHILDREN.—Eliza S——— was charged with deserting her infant children, Rachel aged three, and Susan aged two years, whereby they had become chargeable to the Guardians of the parish of St. George-in-the-East.—Mr. John Barnes, one of the relieving officers, said that the children were brought to the workhouse by a police constable on the 13th September last, and they had been chargeable ever since at a cost to the Guardians of £13 10s.—The prisoner, in reply to the charge, said that she did not desert the children. She left them on the bed with the father. He took them out and put them down somewhere, and watched them until a policeman took them away to the workhouse.—In answer to the magistrate, Mr. Barnes said that the prisoner's husband only died twelve months ago.—Mr. De Rutzen sentenced her to three months' with hard labour.

THE PARROT-KEEPER'S GUIDE,
BY AN EXPERIENCED DEALER

That it is necessary to slit a parrot's tongue to enable it to talk
is fallacious. Caress the bird. Indulge it with sponge-cake fancies,
bean flowers and strawberries in season,
to produce the desired effect.

A Ring-necked Parakeet requires a patient tutor.
If not taken in hand very young it will learn nothing,
content to pass through life lacking accomplishments
like many an idle girl.

The African Parrot receives the lessons of its teacher
with docility and grace. Apropos of the female Love Bird:
a more surly, ill-tempered little glutton never existed.
She rips out her husband's feathers.

The vivacity of Bengal Parakeets is charming when they perform
their little exercises, their perfect *As-tu déjeuné, Cocotie?*
But they will too often persist in their own speech –
a disagreeable, incessant screeching.

The female Groffins Cockatoo is demure but dull.
I have kept one that never mastered more than two words,
Well and *Martha* repeated in a low timid voice.
The latter was her own name.

Eggs of the Paradise Parrot are white. Turn one in your hand.
So perfect in itself – like a full moon that does nothing
but widen the icy distances over our rooftops.
The shell has a faint lustre, as of marble.

A case of greenshank

The light is quiet and used-up, faded by distance. Evening light after rain, transparent grey, yellow to the west. A dusting of gold on the air.

A loch, silvery and perfectly flat. Gauzy mountains slope down to the water, floating in the pause before dusk begins to thicken.

Close to the glass, two wire-legged birds are composed in an arrangement of twigs. Their feathers are sleek, stippled like lichen and stone, their black eyes alert. They have turned their heads. There is no sign of disturbance, but something out of sight on the shore has caught their attention.

Three young men are tying up a rowing boat. They will gather their hunting bags and their guns and set off down the track to a lodge where a gong will be struck for dinner. One will remark that the sky has cleared and tomorrow will be fine.

And this is what two of them will talk about when they return years later: the gauzy mountains, the light on the loch. And how the next day was fine, but by then they were on the train, rattling south.

The birds will never leave for their wintering grounds.

Hummingbirds

Five hummingbirds: confections of feather and wire, like fishing flies.

Each bird is mounted on a wooden peg, as if a child could wind a handle and the automata would bob their heads and flap their stiff wings. Trictrac. A hummingbird's heart beats a thousand times a minute.

What does it mean to inhabit so intensely the space of a minute?

Skins

After prayers for the guide they had buried in a clearing, they supervised the stowage of tents and nailed shut crates for the journey downriver. For weeks they carried the forest in their bodies. Peppery green air folded into their sleep; they dreamed green-lit paths through the understorey. Little chirruping frogs were scarlet alarm clocks.

Wednesday, 5am. Sharp whistles, trills. An enchanting call of 'Eeh o lay and where are you?' Bold whistles, repeated. Tin trumpet.

Months later at the museum they opened crates of feathery pouches stuffed with straw. Each bird had been emptied of its body, dusted with arsenic powder and skewered before it was packed for travel. Lungs, eyes and voice box discarded. Now the birds were furled umbrellas. Military standards. Jumping jacks. Wings could flap open like notebooks. Now the birds were mnemonics for birds.

Eeh o lay and where are you? a bird called in the clearing.

They tied labels to the legs: species, place, date of death. The name of the man who had shot it. Now the histories of birds could begin.

WEST INDIA DOCK

a Provident Legislature
the Corporate Body
Complete SECURITY

STABILITY, INCREASE AND ORNAMENT

THE RIGHT HONOURABLE
THE RIGHT HONOURABLE
under the favour of GOD

ILLUSTRIOUS

rums   mahoganies   dye-woods
sugar warehouses   crystallising sugar*   its lustre

*free-grown in casks
slave-grown in boxes   distinct

O barley-sugar temples   O dainties

riches of the universe poured at her proud feet

100,000 tons at the Import Dock
4 men winching each crane
walls 20 foot high   iron gates   a guardhouse
Weighers & Searchers
counting houses mounted on wheels

CONTRIVANCES & BONDS

Mr Hibbert, plantation owner
West India merchant upwards of forty years:
the plunderer is very ingenious

BIRD-DEALER'S WIFE

Eliza

At night she listens to grass parakeets
in their cages, a room full of rain
sluicing across sleep

in all the colours of panic. He tells her
how the *Lydia* set sail from Brisbane
so crammed with gaudy shrieking birds

that two weeks out sailors turned mutinous –
like a ship full of women –
flung two or three hundred loose

a swarm of rosellas, turquoisines,
rainbow lorikeets, reeling out into dazzle.
She knows the crew must have looked back

only once, silent. Every morning
he lays out trays of finches and sunbirds,
counts them into his death book.

THE LONDON CAGE

The workmanship's in the securing of wires,
the exactness of fastenings.
Tiny red spiders will hide in loose joints.

Nothing more distressing to the cage-maker
than a badly wired cage.

A London Cage, well-made:
now that's *a business-like article.*
One or two compartments, a small nursery
secluded from the living quarters by a door.
An independent tenement, plain as possible.
A well-ordered system. A cage
pleasing to find in a working man's home
as a cheerful wife, a clean hearth
and an eight-day clock

and no weak points in the mesh that could be disclosed
by a slant of blue air between rooftops,
early morning, a sudden smell of bread. A boy
running barefoot without a sound,
the neighbour who looks up from stamping turf
over a hole he has dug the size of a barrel
without a sound
                    and without a sound
shouts news of one army or another.

A MAP OF ROADS AND NAVIGABLE WATERS

He is a young man, and there must be a boat.

He has walked north from a country that does not yet exist.
He has three dates of birth.
He has a name in three languages.

A name in three languages is a boat
(barca   batellu   bagoù)
a space to live in
and the trace it braids through a map.

He climbs out of a boat at a flight of watermen's stairs.

Perhaps Irongate Stairs (no trace now)
where for centuries a skiff   lighter   steamer
sways in the current,
all its tenses held at the stand of the tide

which soon will begin to roll back towards a dock
crowded with people who are always getting closer
or becoming smaller and smaller
until there is nothing to look back to but blue sea or grey.

Ahead of him, his stories are flickers and shadows.
Only these stairs, slippery with river mud, are certain
and the orange I have put in his knapsack –
an orange he will eat tomorrow, walking along the black wharves.

Thursday, twenty-ninth of January
and he's waiting at the court house in Portugal Street –

something about Insolvent Debtors,
Petitions and Process. Something like a dead weight
lodged under the ribs,
the last good black clothes frayed at the wrists –

his name there, between William Dodds, Dealer in Coals
and Mary Swire, formerly of Constantinople,
of no business or occupation.

       And *at Eleven o'Clock precisely*
he steps forward into the light: Gaetano
(who is also Gaspard, also George)

now and for twenty-three years past
of Ratcliffe Highway, Saint George's-in-the-East.

Strike up the band! Fanfaronade!
Importer and Dealer in Foreign Birds and Curiosities,
Bird Cage Maker.
                      Applause!

For one minute precisely he stands in the light.

William Dodds looks up from his scribbled arithmetic.
Mary Swire remembers how a bolt of peacock silk
slid through her fingers.

Then she's gone
and the Dealer in Coals has gone, and the Bird Cage Maker,
and the clerk in the darkening room has stopped writing.

CHILDREN'S SONG

my father whistled to the river
and a ship came in
its sails spread like wings
parakeets as bright as fruit
swayed on all its masts

my mother pinned green feathers in her hair
she turned and laughed
she danced
but bad luck spun a coin that night
wind swung to the east

and my father took us by the hand
he walked us by the river
and he left us there together
like the seashells in his shop
he arranges on pretty beds of moss

THE TUNE HE HEARD ON VINEGAR STREET

The one remaining frame of a lost film,
its noise long-decayed into air.
A crowded street, no one noticing the camera reeling them in

and this nothing-happening caught at the margin:
a shadow in a doorway. A trick of old light.

It's early September.
It could be an afternoon of warm bricks, dusty sunlight
but all the time in the day has tightened into a knot

and watched them until.

The street hurries on.

Round and round the one remaining frame of this film,
the street hurries on, no one going anywhere

while there in the middle of the crowd –
and perhaps this was important once –
a small boy plays an inaudible penny whistle.

CHILDREN'S SONG

when my father spoke we became very small
fierce as wrens
we held very still
in the white stones and thistles
of our father's tongue
we crept under rain among lost things
a hook and an eye and a twist of wire
a bird's grey feather and its white bones

when my father spoke he ruled restless air
he locked cross-wires
to binding wires
he filled cages with white stones and thistles
we saw the brass key he had lost on the road
we saw it all with our quick eyes
the key and the lock and the cage full of rain
and the bird flown out of its bones

THE PRISONER SAID

Charged with deserting her two infant children,
Rachel, aged three and Susan, aged two
whereby they had become chargeable to the Guardians
at a cost of £13 and 10 shillings

The prisoner said

Silt clots her mouth,
blooms in her lungs.
Something distant is happening to her,
a great ship passing
fathoms above.

The prisoner said
she did not desert them.

She left them on the bed with the father.
He took them out somewhere
and watched until

And then they are gone, simply
as if they had been snatched on the wind,
their small dirty feet dangling,
the crowd stock-still, every face a pond full of sky
until a seller of clockwork birds drops his tray
and the street shakes itself back to commotion,
trampling the last tinny wingbeats
like a scene of bad news sent from home.

The prisoner said

the only words she spoke in her life
that anyone recorded,
pressed into lead.

What moves through her
is invisible, silent
as the dark between stars.

A DEMONSTRATION

A bird – a cockatiel, a lark, any small bird –
placed in a glass vessel. A valve closed. An air pump
set at work upon the Exsuction. Pinion and rack
wheeze at their labour and now invisible mountains,
oceans of air, are dragged between the toothed wheels.
The bird droops. Claws scrabble at glass. Pretty chirrups
grow coarse. Convulsions. The air pump pumps on.
Distances clot in the bird's eye. How soon
silence fills the vessel's spaces, as if for eight minutes
all this is happening too far away to be heard.
Then how the bird dies: *her Breast upward, Head downwards,*
her Neck awry as you stand attentive in some remote place
whose air is exactly the shape of any sound,
luscious in the mouth.

ELIZA IN THE LAUNDRY

Eliza widow bird
turn-a-hand-as-needs-must
hand-to-mouth
ask-no-questions Eliza
her face blurred in steam.

Slopping under her hands,
ink-smeared cuffs, tobacco,
oil of violets. A hair
caught on a pearl button,
stained lace.

Somewhere a man will put on clean linen
like expensive forgiveness
or a woman will unfold a gown,
her new life, unsullied and airy
in a room where everything is as it should be

but for one moment
that falls like frost on her skin
and perhaps she will stop
as if something has tilted,
something has been taken.

She said she did not desert the children.

Ask-no-questions Eliza, bent over a tub
scrubs at a girl's white petticoat.
Pushes billowy cotton under water,
a stone in her mouth,
her face blurred in steam.

CHILDREN'S SONG

my father wore translated shoes
his country was a word for Easter bread

that day by the river
he opened both his hands
the river took the silence in
my father turned the key

my father was brass
and his words a locked cage
but my mother was water
and light on water

that glances and darkens
as the wind turns

WOMEN DANCING IN A CIRCLE

For five years the minister has reported
from midnight till 2am beneath his windows
on summer nights

> *bare-headed women*
> *dancing in a circle with language*
> *and attitudes most offensive.*

He rules lines in his journal. Figures
jig and stumble, vanish from reckoning.

Women rescued from degradation:	*270*
Abandoned infants, dead:	*85*
Children not present at our school today:	*60*

The plants he brought from Kent
grow lank and mottled.
> *(Oh the night is dark*
> *and I am far from home.)*

I want to see Eliza flushed and gaudy
arm in arm with these women
who stamp their broken boots
and throw open their wild throats

like those who came forth at evening
from toil in vineyards
singing and dancing with timbrels

their lost children asleep
swaddled in hollows of their hips
their bodies heavy and joyful.

A woman, men in bulky black clothes. A small room
at the end of a tunnel of accordion folds,
intensely close and unreachable.
The men exchange words, build structures
without windows or doors. *Mr John Barnes said.*
The magistrate said. Their high tight collars,
their square backs. Their mouths opening. *She said.*
The prisoner said. The men hand bricks one to the other.
Mr Barnes said *the prisoner's husband*
only died twelve months ago. But the magistrate said.
Nothing else said. Her voice
barely a thread of air behind soot-stained bricks.
So little air in this room that's contracting into itself
closing its accordion folds.

ELIZA, OLD

at sunset she takes off her apron
leaving her body's narrow yards
she walks under a bell of sky

wind strips her small painted words
there is ice on the river her ship
will not come the day burns to cinder

a distant window flowers into light
plain as her tin mug precious
as an egg warm in her hands

she carries its glow cradled soft
in the cup of her hands her care
not a drop spilled not a drop

spilled on the folding ice
as it heaves up its shining back
opens its wide throat and she listens

she listens for what comes to sing her
through the night to walk with her
into last spring's drifting willow pollen

CHILDREN'S SONG

two birds sat on a white stone
they saw it all with their clever eyes
one flew away and then there was one
hidden in thistles and curled brown leaves
the other flew after and then there were none

my mother sings poor stone poor stone
left all alone
my father sings not here not here
far far away
a white road leads down to the sea

DISAPPEARANCES

Somewhere distant, men are emptying trees.
They leave only three-clawed prints that translate as *birds
in flight over a field*. That last until rain.

He keeps his language in a dark house,
feeds it dry biscuit. It shivers, tears out its feathers.
The cage hangs like a broken lamp.

She breathes herself out in three sentences.
Her words are listless and pale. For an hour, her name
runs wild through the streets.

Two small girls walk hand in hand through a forest.
They do not follow a path to a gold-lighted cottage at dusk.
There is no silvery bird, nor its singing bones,

not even an old woman twisted with hunger for a child.
There is no path. Soon it is too cold to walk further
and too dark.

SIGNATURE

In the quiet room where you show your researcher's card, they teach you to wind a reel of microfilm through the reader. A craft skill, like casting on knitting or threading a loom, the half-remembered tension of over and under, turn and loop. Knowledge in shoulder and wrist, the hand's fine bones and tendons.

And then the fabric unrolling
the thick weave of years, days
processions of men and stiff-skirted women
walking arm in arm
red flowers big as cartwheels
under their turned-out feet.

A cloth spread out in the shade
where we might sit together for an hour
to tell our names and our stories
before travelling on.

His signature: child in a schoolroom.
Hers: a scrawled X.

I remember being unable to read. The mesh of knots and loops that concealed voices, gestures, invisible presences. And now I am illiterate again, a traveller in a country whose whole language is written in one letter:

```
      good luck    the fire laid
         a kiss    a wrong answer
        if this    times that
counts on fingers  a crossroads
           here    crossed out
```

Scrap of warp thread latched across weft.

Ghost bodies on a screen, their pressure soft as moths.

Pens are not allowed in the quiet room. You must bring with you as little as possible, and the entrance is difficult to find.

WRITING BACKWARDS TO THE BIRDCAGE MAKER

How long did it take, the journey
from that port where marble lions ripen?

What distance travelled to *the Italian House*
the cages checked morning and evening?
Was that arrival or finally leaving? The watching

    the loosening of hands.

These questions of distance, birdcage maker –

each of us walking through our muddled days
muttering in our own dialect
twisting it into shapes to hold some wild flapping creature
in all its improbable colours.

        On my screen
handwriting hauls its footprints over the snow
hunched into east wind
      and obsearve the
 ... first watch thi ... and obsearve the

The words are written backwards
      ... evraesbo... evraesbo...

a traveller vanishing into the blizzard
who calls back to where – how many days' walk behind? –

I'm searching for a bird flown

   scrape of wind across rock

    a word travelling towards me.

7 December 2018. I am a hundred years too late.

She died a hundred years ago on this day in December, the month when each week slides more deeply into dark. Shorter, shorter, the shortest days, not light until eight, dark by four. London in December 1918 was a city of the damaged and the grieving, hollowed out by war and epidemic, but December is in any case a month when the old fail, and Eliza was very old. She died in Mile End workhouse in a time of common dying and was buried in a common grave. A pauper's death, owning nothing, leaving nothing. And I have come to find her, on a day of sharp light and unseasonal warmth

*

There is a terrain to be travelled in search of the dead, a topography of erosion and fracture. The document missing from an archive, the mistake in a date, the illegible writing. Always the hope that suddenly in a street of locked doors – there, *there* – the concealed entrance, the flight of steps descending into shadow. A way back through years that have fallen like soot, year upon year – and there under tarmac, lost alleys and courts. Inaudible voices coming closer.

A year earlier I had stood outside a petrol station on the Ratcliffe Highway, trying to overlay nineteenth-century house numbers onto a street without houses. Trying to imagine Eliza there, in her Italian husband's house, in a shop crammed with sailors' curios and exotic birds. Perhaps the house was where I stood, or under the supermarket, the takeaway, the flats across the road – a road which seemed too wide to be old, and which hasn't been called the Ratcliffe Highway for over a century.

It was raining and cold, daylight shutting down, and I soon lost interest. I was in the right place, more or less, but the place itself had gone away. Or perhaps it had only gone away from me. The fluorescent sheen of petrol station lights made everything it touched look flimsy and sad.

> *no. 44: John Lush, umbrella maker*
> *no. 59: Mary Commander (Mrs) brushmaker*
> *no. 63: Charles Cusani, wireworker*
> *no. 149: Samuel Samuels, watchmaker*
> *no.176: Mary Wipperman, grocer*

the colour man

the slop seller   the looking glass maker

the Half Moon and Seven Stars

the Artichoke

the Old Rose

*

Stairs, escalators, Tube platform. But this is not the deep underground that tunnels 40 metres, 60 metres, below the city, counting back the full measure of human history. I am travelling close to the surface, barely six metres under traffic and footfall. 'Cut and cover', the civil engineers' term, suggesting a swift, vicious process like Victorian surgery or grave-robbing.

Do what has to be done, hide the damage. Disappear.

A small jolt off balance – this is a route I know, one thread in a tangle of journeys I used to make as a small child with my mother. Places east of the city, north of the river, flicking across display boards, conceal addresses that once bounded my life. Whether this is belonging or distance, I cannot decide. But only now, the past tilted to a new sightline, do I think about the last twenty years of Eliza's life, a laundress in Mile End, seven years in Mile End Workhouse before she died on the far edge of a century I too had inhabited. My grandmother, Eliza's granddaughter, was a child when Eliza died. Eliza was within touching distance of my life.

Almost within touching distance. Six metres below ground is considered sub-surface. Invisible, but so shallow that if your house is built over a Tube line you may feel vibrations of passing trains as you drowse off to sleep. No one had ever told me about Eliza. Cut and cover.

*

Eliza was still a young woman when teams of railway navvies had begun digging through Essex gravel and silt. Within forty years villages out on marshland were already becoming the East London that snags at corners of my mind. As far as I know, I have ever been here before but when I walk out of Plaistow station towards East London Cemetery I know at once these long treeless roads exposed to every wind. Blank houses raw with bruised hopes. Tight brick terraces named for highland excursions and imperial wars. And I know the triangles of brambly scrub, nettles and rosebay, child-height between railings, where an unenclosed place pushes back to the surface, shining in December sun.

Ghosting: *the appearance of a doubled image on a screen, one layer superimposed and offset over the other. Often caused when a signal travels by two different paths, with a slight difference in timing.*

> *sheep grazing among willow*
> *the Tar and Liquor Works*
> *lapwings sharp as sleet over the ploughlands*
> *tide mills and trackways*
> *pools shining like lenses*
> *the smallpox hospital*
> *the Gas Light and Coke Works*

Always, a fugitive, estuarine landscape; more than half the land in the parish lay below the level of spring tides. Things vanished. Smuggled goods were landed in creeks; animals were stolen or lost to fast tides. Human beings, too, could disappear in shifting contours of channels, mist and tide. Outsiders unable to read this fluid language created their own mirror-marsh in narratives of 'black ditches' and 'desolate inns' where 'at dead of night' a trapdoor opens… As if east of the city lay at an edge of the mind where terror waits.

When a road was built across Plaistow Marsh in 1810 the timbers that supported it rotted away.

In the end, the marsh itself vanished; slowly at first, dug out to build the Royal Victoria Dock. It was loaded onto barges and taken upriver to become Battersea Park. Willow pollen, needle-fine bones of curlew, under the multi-sports pitch and the rose garden. What remained disappeared within a lifetime, drained and built over. Ham Creek, once a navigable channel, was occluded. When I first read this, I mistook the word for occulted – but a creek stopped up against the tide does become hidden under the contours of a new map. Sometimes even the memory of what was lost is elusive. An occasional reference to Roman coins, pottery, dug out during nineteenth-century drainage leads nowhere except back to itself. The objects, if they exist, might as well have sunk back into the mud.

*

An engraving of an estuary hung in my grandparents' house. A whispery copperplate caption: *Oh Mary, go and call the cattle home across the sands of Dee.* The picture's desolate sepia light, the words' incomprehensible sadness, held me for years. My grandparents owned little, they saved shillings for the gas meter and kept the rent money safe on the mantelpiece. Why, I think now, did they own this?

> *The rolling mist came down and hid the land*
> *And never home came she.*
> *But still the boatmen hear her call the cattle home*
> *Across the sands of Dee.*

I have no idea what happened to the picture after my grandparents' deaths.

*

There is no one around as I walk these streets to the cemetery, and this too feels familiar; the memories I have of these places float silently, without context. I feel invisible, returning to a place I think I know.

But this is where recognition ends, at the grand double gates of a cemetery. An avenue stretches across lawns that gleam improbably green. Stiff rosebushes still in flower, an entrance lodge with mullioned windows. This could be the entrance to a great country house where you'd live out a lifetime unseen, a skivvy, a slavey. In 1878, Eliza went to prison accused of abandoning her two youngest daughters, aged three and two. They were taken to the workhouse. After that, no trace of their existence. They probably died small anonymous deaths like many workhouse children. If they survived fevers and infections, this would have been their lives, sent into service, too young to carry with them any memory of who they had been. Their names would have been changed if their employers so chose. Cut and cover.

And now, in this neat place, where death is close and too bright, I no longer know why I am here. How can anyone know about a woman, one of thousands, who died a century ago leaving hardly a trace of her presence in the world? I open the door of the lodge.

There are flowers on the counter; two women busy at computers. Of course, one says, unsurprised. She types Eliza's name and the date of her death. Beside me, a man asks about a rosebush to be planted on his father's grave. The woman is still typing, scrolling. Frowning. Eliza won't be found, I'm sure of this now, she's got away, slipped through the datasets. I'm a hundred years too late and I've wandered into a landscape that could drown you. The woman crosses the office, hands me a yellow Post-it note. A plot number. I have found her.

There's nothing to see, she says, a nurse breaking bad news. Nothing there. The grave plots were re-used.

I hadn't imagined this, and I don't want to ask about the re-use of grave plots, not here, standing next to a man who cannot decide between red or yellow roses. Can I go and look anyway, look for something, even if I have no idea what it is I won't see?

*

I walk beyond the rosebushes, some hung with Christmas decorations. A stone dog sleeps at the foot of a gravestone, there is a stone dartboard and a stone football. Not a country house; a neighbourhood of the dead where it's always the weekend. The path winds between Chinese graves. Someone has placed a bowl of oranges on one, a gift luminous with loss. English inscriptions: born in Shanghai. Born in Canton, born in Poplar, in Stepney. I like the narrow columns of gold text, off-centred like poems on a page – and because I cannot read these texts, I read instead symmetries and rhythms in chisel cuts, tapering flicks and upstrokes. If I stared long enough, perhaps I could unpack each character, understand fine distinctions.

I am close to the perimeter now, I can see a boundary fence, tower blocks beyond it. On one side of the path, hundreds of sturdy nineteenth-century graves jostle like people in a park listening to the brass band. Ernests and Agathas. Adèle, Emil, Jane, Hanne; gilded, granite names. And here, on the other side, trees lay long traceries of shadow across a field of small gravestones, some leaning, some almost hidden in grass as if they were sinking. There are no decorated graves, no statues. It feels like an older, forgotten place, a country churchyard out of its time. Last summer's leaves lie curled in rough grass. I do not know if I should walk off the path, but how else will I find her?

Ghosting. *See also* After image: *an optical illusion of an image that continues to appear in one's vision after exposure has ceased.*

See also Spirit photography: *an attempt to capture an image of a ghost.*

*

I want Eliza to be here, to have quiet seasons under the trees, after the prison, the laundry, the workhouse. The grass is muddy, uneven between the headstones – like grave mounds, a sanctuary, somewhere more ancient than a churchyard. I begin to look for plot numbers. The gravestones, I realise, are less old than they appear, hardly more than sixty years, lined up in wide-spaced rows that wander slightly out of true. I walk up and down each row like a water diviner, holding out my Post-it note. I think I must be close, the numbers are climbing towards me. I keep walking, stooping to numbers carved on the backs of headstones, and now they are receding, I can no longer understand the sequence and I have no idea in which direction to turn. But I know that soon, any moment, I will brush away leaves and read the number cut into stone. I know this has to happen, I can see it, in the way you can see where a lost key should be, and so you return to the place again and again, disbelieving its absence.

Of course I do not find her. I think: she was sent to prison for deserting her children. The only imprint she left on the world is a few words she spoke in court, denying the charge. Perhaps she was telling the truth. Perhaps she was lying. Why would she not? She was sent to prison anyway. The children vanished. Everything about this story is unknowable. When I retell it, it gives out not a glimmer of light, but only reflects the listener and the teller, changing in the different weathers they inhabit, like those pools where travellers drowned when fog closed in. I think: she couldn't be trusted. She has given me the slip.

But someone has left a small bunch of flowers under a tree and I photograph that – the leafless tree against ice-blue sky, the flowers, the muddy grass laced with shadows.

IN THE MARSH COUNTRY

Map

trying to recall a tune	drift line decoy pond
a ripple through the lode	
a slant in the colour of water	gravel mud shell bank
not a tune yet	
sounding the shape	3.0 2.0 3.2 0 -2 -2.6
a shoal moving under skin	
shadow island	[covers at high water]
someone finding a way	
fluctuating channel	marked by withies
across permeable borders	
through a body of water	fish weir [remains of]
tomorrow in altered light	
contours will have drifted	4 3.6 2.0 0 -3 0
a ragged flight of geese	
hollowing out dusk	Iron Age mound [trace of]
someone on the sea wall	
walking back to a lighted window	house [site of]
trying to recall a tune	

Fleet, high tide, 10pm

Two hares running across a field. A hare
and the thought of a hare fleeting its shadow.

Evening star over the fleet. Flimmers under water.
A ritual of floating lights, flame small as a soul
travelling through dark.

A star, the pin this night turns on.
Our flight towards winter.

Old Hall Marshes

I come out of the house You are there on the sea wall I walk

round to the gate A broken sign Footpath to Sea Wall

lies in the grass points back to the house You have vanished

Turn at the path Four wooden steps to the wall No sign of you

Walk round the empty wharf Basement mud Grasses tick

A silver bead A shiver in the balance Two miles away

tide running in A runnel Slides back through sloughed coils

Sightlines heel round Another turn I see you again The house

low under sky The marsh slow breathing itself into water

Fingringhoe, St Margaret of Antioch

The saint in a broken niche
nurses her heavy book at her breast.

Someone hated her eyes –
how her indrawn gaze walked

circuitous tracks through the marsh
into sea's manifold language. *Antioch.*

We have nowhere to be but in words.
Antioch cold water at her ankles.

Smashed her face. One clean slash
right eye to left cheekbone.

Her mouth undamaged
and her large competent hands.

Bradwell Power Station (Decommissioned)

no visible entrance or exit
slab and cube swept by aluminium light

silver / grey / citrine at dusk
each day's parabola as it falls

leaves its soft chaff   shadow traces
in flow across a white screen

[Rauschenberg: I called them clocks]

sealed in safestore time burns away
to a pinprick   an eyelet into dark

where someone driving through the night
sees for an instant a running creature

drawn out of air   caught in flight
for an instant   backlit by radiance

Pillbox

is a cistern full of listening.

White noise in the grass.

Winches & lifting rings
barbed tangles.
Blackberry, blackthorn
heaping over. Concertina wire
could be. Light passes across
three observation slits
which are also gun slits
& admit no light
no observing.

(Hardened Defences.
Impossible to approach unseen.)

Listen in. Throw in a pebble.
Depth sounding.

A detonation. Three crows
shatter out of dark
& nowhere under blank sky
to crouch in the lee of
while air corrugates over your head.

A car moves along the track
behind the sea wall

behind the jolt of a car approaching.

Dengie

Now the reckoning. Straw-bales blocked against the sea wall.
Smoke idles over a stubble field. Three attendants walk in a slow circle –

there is a wild thing that wants to break from their implements,
to run through the stubble. An unfenced field to the horizon

and three circling. Their bright shirts. We drive past
taking it with us like an unopened letter. In all my photographs, sky

tilts towards the sea, there is nothing to hold back its spill
across ditches and concrete roads, fields

thoughts keep slipping through into the margins
to grub at nettles, cans full of rainwater. Sometimes feathers, small bones.

August 2019

SOUTHEND

       something promised
no one can draw it because it never stops moving
words dissolved now in dusty sunlight

which must be a hot afternoon
               a road I am watching unroll
towards this thing no lines can contain
that paces to and fro outside the perimeter   crying out
twisting and clenching its hands
                  crying out

             but what happens is two miles of damp sand
which could not have been deserted that hot day
but are now empty and silent and only sand
stretched tight across earth's curve
               myself barefoot
perhaps a red plastic bucket in hand
               myself walking barefoot
across the absence of what had been promised
not wanting anything
           but this not wanting

and two miles away
       a thread is ravelling between silver and grey

       the slippery edge of a thought
       which that day had kept its distance

       leaving everything

           perfectly wordless

ROTHERHITHE

What I find at the foot of Prince's Stairs at low tide

Neck of a bottle
                        freckled earthenware
                        plump as a song thrush

Chunk of fogged glass
                        moulded nubs and trails
                        unreadable under my fingertips

Five-sided lozenge of willow pattern
                        a houseboat
                        a cupped hand with a cabin on its palm

Elsewhere on this plate scenes from a toy operetta
all happen at once on miniature islands
a woman   a lover   a murderous father

                then two birds
like lapwings tumbling together

                not a wingspan of air between them

But I find only the boat and a man's legs   knees bent
because he is leaning his weight to the long oar
that will push his boat on   away
                            over the lake

All these pocked and blurred
                        I thumb their edges
feel for sharp angles
            but the river has ground away their exactness

Impossible to believe
we never touch anything

We make it all up out of particles
a shimmer at the boundary   a story
that travels on the tides

and so we must be alone
each in our own desert place that fits close
as air fits to the flex of a wing

Wind passes through a wire fence   we translate *river*
                        birds calling

We translate   *take my hand dearest   touch my hair*

            we are home

Or not home but near as the voice to its echo

The river wall has grown a thin pelt   emerald green
hung with chains
A woman's voice flickers at the edge of a conversation
drifting down from streets high above

I have dropped into river time   flint and mud
and the river widening

beyond warehouse conversions   depots and cranes

Albion Wharf   Greenland Dock   Cathay Street

              he   she

                    I

Flint pebble

                    mottled orange and black   perfectly smooth
                              tiny planet

Oyster shells   their growth-years worn to sharp disks

                    pearly like watered silk

                              a mirage of sea

EITHER AN EYEPIECE OR A CORRECTING LENS

How towering cliffs resolve to boulders or a new horizon
transfixes a ship for hours sailing nowhere,

how Arctic air unhooks time from distance (coordinates adrift,
the eye climbing spires and promontories everywhere at once)

and how at 6pm on a Thursday in January
three watermen were riding the ebb tide to Greenland Dock –

sleet then snow, the river obsidian, devouring itself
and they the only men left alive in a cosmos of whirling flint

that begins to warp now, to slow, until the machinery locks.
Inside the cathedral air of the icefield they hear weights rise and fall,

glass chains run through pulleys. Steel gates drop into place.
Ice shines up at their faces, unblinking.

Hours later they sat in the King of Prussia, staring into a fire
as if they had returned after years from a continent of mirrors,

unable to speak of the silver chronometers scattered on the floe,
the message written backwards to the dead, the ships in the sky.

THE HUMAN VOICE FROM A DISTANCE

The oldest recording of a human voice:
a machine invented by a typographer.
An April day in 1860 and for twenty seconds
a man sings *Au clair de la lune*

as if he threw back his head in a burnt-out city
and lifted his hands to the sky. He sings
Pierrot répondit into onrushing wind.
Great trees are torn down in the boulevards.

His voice is etched into lampblack
and now his song is a black-sailed ship
bearing its burden through breaking waves
bearing on through the night.

O mon ami Pierrot what awaits us in the dark?
Give me your pen
give me soot from your lantern
to write our passing into air.

We rock in our small boats
singing like a storybook in the moonlight
Ma chandelle est morte
Je n'ai plus de feu.

Our wake widens into ocean behind us
until we see only debris
floating on oily water.

IN EARLY PHOTOGRAPHS, BUSY STREETS
APPEAR DESERTED

And because no one has yet invented shutter speeds
it is a peaceful city
where light falls with the silvery quiet of snow
taking no less than several minutes to land
and shadows lie unperturbed by passers-through.
There are no starlings. No one runs to a dying woman's house
and it is never windy.

Sometimes a man stands, one foot raised
struck by the devotion of a child
who kneels to polish his boot.
Should two or three people happen to meet at a street corner
they stop to look into each other's eyes
as if to say, This is all our life
gathered here inside this room, the curtains kept closed

while elsewhere perhaps a theatre is on fire
and streets fly into a thousand pieces
overtaking the minute hand on every white-faced clock
but only now do you see
a woman who turns aside in her own still air
transfixed by clouds the colour of lead
solidifying in a cage of black roofbeams.

TRANSIT CIRCLE

the river brings back what it takes   lost things
orbit in its currents
                    until something of them returns

a flower on a flake of china
                    a pattern recollected
in the space between tides

                    mother   or daughter
                    In fond

in Greenwich the Airy Transit Circle
stands in imaginary zero time
from which everything else is imagined

a roof slides open   the telescope locks to a star

every second the chronograph marks time on a roll of paper

                    *

                         *

                              *

trace of a passing through
                    observances kept

as if translated shapes
                        misheard syllables
voicings across shingle and mud

might be salvage
                        an opened border

while beyond the estuary mouth
                        the river begins to turn over

                                Oaze Deep

                                Barrow Deep

                                Black Deep

ZUGUNRUHE

First named in 1817 by Johann Andreas Naumann
who observed, as skies above his beet fields
sagged with first snow,
the golden oriole in his bird room

1. wing-fluttering while perched
2. restlessness at dusk
3. beating (always south) against the cage at night
4. hunger.

Concluded
migration is rooted in the nature of the bird
but did not record opening the cage
nor standing by the casement to watch his oriole
flash across acres of black tilth, over plantations,
its *fast undulating flight*
true as the travel between sunlight and sunlight.

For twenty years *alte Naumann*
worked on his natural history of German birds,
crumbed soil between thumb and forefinger
as all Naumanns had, walking their bounds
down to the river where barges passed
into the noise of elsewhere:
its flags and its drums, its limping stragglers
hauling barrows along frozen tracks.

A MAP OF THE WORLD

One aunt could remember her old people
who didn't speak her language. They wore black,
she said, always black.

One uncle remembered his father going back with a key
and his papers. He returned with a pencil box
they'd given him, for the boy.

One cousin remembered a road. The other
refused to remember. The metal pins in her leg
ached at night.

And there's my neighbour who dug up his vines
and boarded a train with roots wrapped in newspaper
under his coat,

my friend who burnt his passport and hated the cold
and my friend who went back for her revolution.
She never phoned.

All of them, treading desire paths in a country of between,
listening to what shifts underfoot. Their shadows overlap,
sitting late at kitchen tables

or on Sundays in bus stations at the edge of small towns
where the fountains have rusted. Cement dust drifting,
a few dead leaves

restless, then still, and one hand passes into another
a suitcase of faded photographs, recipes, account books,
letters to unknown addresses.

A STORY

He sits down beside me at the ferry port, uninvited.
Uninvited, he begins to empty his rucksack of books. Urgent and precise,

dealing out books on white flagstones. Do you want this one?
Look at this one. Prayer books, Somali cookery. Children's puzzles –
wordsearches, find hidden animals.

I do not want books. I do not want puzzles or prayers.

In this sea light where everything is fizzing out of its edges
I do not want to search for what's lost.

The boy waits.

This book with a photograph on its cover: a man's thin silhouette
wading through sea foam. He carries a long spar of wood along a beach.
The spar looks like an oar. Like a winnowing fan.

I open a page. *When we arrived in Ancona it rained.*
If it rains when you reach a new country, that means good luck.

He takes my euros. Snaps shut his fan of books
and now there is only white stone, the sun-scarred Adriatic,
a book in my hand

and what he says before he walks away, fast,
might have been *This is my story*, but he spoke very quietly.

GOLDFINCHES

I want to say it's not the fort's blind walls,
the derelict lighthouse, not the tight heat
(whose chained dog, whose empty car?)
but this locked gate on the Hill of Thistles
where air turns on its rim
and the path ends at a field of white stones –

the fact of them, mineral memory.
Light rolling over the sea.

For two long June days
at the foot of this cliff, twenty-four men
and one woman, not native to this city,
not native enough, were hanged and burned.
Or perhaps burned alive. Smoke holds no shape
but this was centuries ago
in an age of countable numbers
and each man was written into ceremony.
The woman's name was not written

and the path ends at a locked gate, white stones.

I want to say I felt air quiver, then swell like a sail
once, in a field, not this field – goldfinches,
twenty perhaps, scattered out of thistles.
Their flicker and dash, their bright dash,
their spark. Their blood-dipped carnival masks.

Their brightness, I want to say,
their small ravenous brightness.

Monte Cardeto, Ancona

SILVER PLATING, GILDING,
RESTORATION TO NEW LIFE

The street compresses shade, a damp-walled passage
cut through the day's fierce blue.

Blank walls, barred windows

                no light admitted. None granted.

Only this door

Specialists in Chromework. Silver Plating, Gilding.
Ripristino a nuova vita

                     shining

the way sunlight pours between two roofs
and for an hour goldens a square of concrete floor
between a stack of boxes and a broken chair.

        An opened space inside the dark
                   a timer ticking down.

The certain moment electric current arcs across a tank –

             what it touches, lightstruck.

Chains, taps, exhausts and tarnished valves
                     raised, pristine

components for some vast musical instrument
that will play waves and moons, ferries going out at night

        spilling silver through the water.

      Via Ciriaco Pizzecolli, Ancona

FINCANTIERI

Two of us on a dock wall
narrow as a roof ridge,
dizzy with salt light. Stone sparking
like salt underfoot. No horizon,
only this glitter vibration
without centre or boundary

but when we look back we see
Fincantieri's red gantry
framing a slab of bright blue –
a foreground of iron rails,
vertebrae, fins. A deadweight
splayed under cables and hooks.

Nothing moves. Silence has settled
like the seconds after catastrophe
or a composition perfected:
Blue sea and sunlight
or *Shipyard*
with two watching figures

until a cyclist in dockyard hi-vis
swings out through the arch.
Shadows flick on his back
as if this were a road between trees
and ahead, a garage with a red door,
a ladder, an orchard.

Lungomare Vanvitelli, Ancona

ABOUT TIME

'Our language differentiates geometries in space and time that may not be different'

and so when a woman in the cemetery office
writes a grave-plot number on a yellow Post-it note
(*but there's nothing to see there*)
I take it from her hand as if it were the gift of a torch
to light me through tunnels
where my voice will go ahead into the dark, returning
on a thread of cold air.
And then, between a path and a fence – not a grave
but a breath exhaled between numbers –
a few bare trees shining black in low sun,
shadow branches webbed over rough grass.
An after-image I cannot blink away:
a grazing meadow, summer. A gathering. My own shade
lying down under the trees.

'We experience time as passing because we move so slowly'

catch the moment / catch the light
catch a woman's face in a crowd

catch her glance / catch her likeness
in the beam of your torch

catch her unawares / catch her out
but the crowd is walking away

too many they are walking too fast
how to catch sight of one woman

catch up / catch your breath
they keep their steady distance

not once do they look back
catch the drift / here's the catch

catch her eye / catch your death
catch the light / catch the light in its fall

'Time is a process of coming into being'

not a memorial stone   a story
neither remembered   nor imagined
a saltwater creek   its vagaries
silt-water   silk-mud   mirror-mud

its vagrancy   *o call*   mist
bends the distances   what's coming
comes in voices   *o call the cattle home*
ripples down a channel   *o call*

its fugitive shallows   its silt-shoals
white curlew bones   pollen-drift
riddled through a map   the half-known

folded in shadows   mist over mirror-water
breath on a mirror   when she died
she left nothing   not even her death

CORSET SHOP WINDOW IN THE EAST END

Outlasts patched and swollen bodies:
their armour, steeled and buckled.
How they scythe on
through breaking seas
these figurehead women. Oh
but the bruised wet heart bound in its hull
the hoarded shillings.
Oh *Mignonne Miranda Nymph*
molasses and pineapples, smoke
curling over the river.
A poster calls hey girl Tonite
Dance Dance Dance.

And at first light the river opens its doors
the foreshore lies glistening
scattered with ribbons
and broken mirrors.
Think of Eliza, think her
glancing shadow
in shadows of big-bellied shirts
cool hollows of sheets in full sail
across Dock Street, light on her face
fanning open and shut.
Oh girl *Hecate Circe Medea*
riding the tideway into the eye of the wind.

DESERTING CHILDREN.—Eliza S—— was charged with deserting her infant children, Rachel aged three, and Susan aged two years, whereby they had become chargeable to the Guardians of the parish of St. George-in-the-East.—Mr. John Barnes, one of the relieving officers, said that the children were brought to the workhouse by a police constable on the 13th September last, and they had been chargeable ever since at a cost to the Guardians of £13 10s.—The prisoner, in reply to the charge, said that she did not desert the children. She left them on the bed with the father. He took them out and put them down somewhere, and watched them until a policeman took them away to the work-house.—In answer to the magistrate, Mr. Barnes said that the prisoner's husband only died twelve months ago.—Mr. De Rutzen sentenced her to three months' with hard labour.

p. 5 *East London Observer*, 15 June 1878.

p. 7 *The Parrot-Keeper's Guide by an Experienced Dealer*, 1851;
W.T. Greene, *Parrots in Captivity*, 1883.

p. 10 Text taken from plaque on the wall of West India Dock;
sugar, barley-sugar temples, riches of the universe,
counting houses, from George Sala, *The Hours of the
Day and Night in London* (1859); 'The plunderer' from
statements made by George Hibbert, plantation owner
and Chairman of the West India Dock Company.

p. 11 'a room full of rain': based on Frank Buckland's description
of hearing caged grass parakeets in *Curiosities of Natural
History*, 1868.

p. 12 Draws on 'Cage-making', in W.A. Blakston, *The
Illustrated Book of Canaries and Cage Birds*, 1878.

p. 21 Robert Boyle, Experiment 41, 1744.

p. 23 'translated shoes': old shoes repaired and sold as new.
Henry Mayhew, Letter xxxv, 1850.

p. 24 Based on material at www.stgitehistory.org.uk and www.
victorianlondon.org.

p. 32 Relics of Sir John Franklin's last Arctic expedition, 1845–
8, National Maritime Museum, Greenwich. Object ID
AAA2114: 'Leather wallet containing... two sheets of
paper with a narrative written backwards.'

p. 44 [We have] 'nowhere to be but in words': Bejan Matur,
'The Island, Myself and the Laurel', in *In the Temple of a
Patient God*, trans. Ruth Christie. Arc, 2004.

p. 45 'I called them clocks': Robert Rauschenberg on his
White Paintings.

p. 52 Relics of Sir John Franklin's last Arctic expedition, 1845–
8, National Maritime Museum, Greenwich. Object ID

AAA2185: 'This lens in a brass mount is from a telescope and is either an eyepiece or one of the correcting lenses'.

p. 53 Édouard-Léon Scott de Martinville, phonautograph recording of 'Au clair de la lune', 1860.

p. 59 'When we arrived in Ancona': Bay Mademba, *Il mio viaggio della speranza*, Giovane Africa Edizioni, 2011.

p. 66 From a photograph by John Claridge, 1960s.

ACKNOWLEDGEMENTS

Versions of some of these poems were first published in *The Fortnightly Review*, *The Interpreter's House*, *Pennine Platform*, *The Rialto*, *Shearsman*, *Strix* and *Tears in the Fence*. My thanks to the editors of those magazines.

Part of 'Rotherhithe' was set for soprano and piano by Alex T. Barker for performance at Leeds Lieder international festival in April 2020.

'About time' is based on words spoken by Professor David Berman and Professor Fay Dowker in the artist Grace Weir's video installation *Time Tries All Things*, Institute of Physics, London 2019. I am grateful to Grace Weir for permission to draw on her work.

Ella Wilson's expertise unlocked archives and gifted me the source of this book. A short conversation with Barry Taylor began to unlock the Thames for me. I am grateful to both. My thanks to editors Michael Schmidt and John McAuliffe, and to all at Carcanet. Thanks, above all, to my family, who are silent companions in some of these poems, and to Sarah Hymas, Carola Luther and Helen Tookey.